For enquiries:
email: info@hachiweli.com
Instagram: @hachiweli
Facebook: @hachiweli

ISBN 978-1-8384968-0-7
Published by:
Rising Star Publishing,
United Kingdom.

Acknowledgement
I would like to thank my mum and dad - Dr and Mrs Weli for encouraging me to write this book. I also want to thank my siblings, grandparents, uncles, aunties, teachers and friends. I wrote this book to share it with you.

CHAPTER 1
"GOLD HUNT"

There were two sisters named Ella and Sophie. Ella was 10 and Sophie was 13. The girls wanted to find some gold but they knew their mum would not let them go on any adventures alone. As soon as they said "gold", their mum went nuts and said, "here take some food and don't be long". The girls left the house and went on their adventure.

CHAPTER 2
MANOR RAGE!

They climbed over mountains and hills. They rolled on and off valleys and swam through raging rivers. Ella began to limp and complain. "I'm tired of walking, let's just go home". "We either go home or we take photos of some gold" bellowed Sophie. "Okay, gold," said Ella.

They walked another mile and then they saw it. In the forest, there was a manor and this old giant house belonged to bears. The manor was made of gold. The Queen of Bears was named Eliza. When they got to the giant door, there were guards but the girls did not know.

They ran through corridors and peeked into doors of many kinds. They came back to the hallway and saw a door that they had not tried. The girls happily went into the room but heard loud sounds coming close to them.

CHAPTER 3
GROWLING ESCAPE

The poor girls were being chased by the harsh looking guard bears. The guards loved to argue a lot. The girls were surrounded by the guards but soon the guards started to argue. It was the girls' only chance to escape so they did.

The girls ran for their lives, they fled into the noisy nursery. There was crying, roaring and growling. "What can we do?" cried Ella, "don't worry" answered Sophie "we can do this!"

CHAPTER 4
NOISY NURSERY

The girls trembled with fear as they hid underneath a cot. The nursery would have been a perfect place to hide in if there were not baby bears babbling and crying in it.

The girls got very annoyed by the noise, soon the noise got even noisier. Ella was so angry that she could not help but shout, "stop this nonsense will you!".

Every baby bear in the nursery glared at Ella and they all growled in hunger. "What can we do?" cried Ella. "Same plan as always, run!" shouted Sophie. They ran and ran until they bumped into the guard bears.

CHAPTER 5
HOT ON THE TAIL

Sofia and Ella were running as fast as they could while the guards were not far behind. The girls scrambled under a gate and found a stable to hide in. The smelly stable was awful. Meanwhile, the guards were still looking for the girls. A guard bear went up the chimney and found nothing but a rat as it ran to get all his luggage and fled.

The rat disappeared into thin air and the bear growled in disappointment. As he climbed down the sooty chimney, he fell into a fire and yelled in pain. The other bear laughed loudly and the bear felt embarrassed.

Back in the stable, the girls were getting very bored until they found a puppy, it was a Golden Terrier. The girls and the puppy got hungry, then the girls remembered the bag their mum gave them. The girls reached for the bag and found a container.

The container was stuffed with ham sandwiches. The girls took out the ham from the sandwiches and gave it to the puppy. After everyone was full, Sophie had a look outside of the stable gate. It was clear, so the girls and the puppy scrambled under the gate and met Queen Eliza with two guards by her side.

CHAPTER 6
FRIENDS WITH THE QUEEN!

The guards were just about to attack when the Queen noticed the worried puppy. She shouted, "stop!". The guards stopped, "Do not lay a hand on them" the Queen said. "They found my puppy," she said.

The Queen wanted the girls to be her friends because they found her puppy. The girls became the Queen's friends. Queen Eliza showed the girls the golden chariots and then showed them the golden garden.

The girls took a picture which they loved so much. They also took a golden flower as a souvenir. When the girls wanted to leave the Manor, the Queen said, "come back and come with your own puppy and family". The girls said, "Au revoir" which is goodbye in French.

CHAPTER 7
BACK AT
HOME

The girls went home safely. At home, their mum, Anne and dad, Brian were very proud of them and they had a party. The girls were also proud of themselves. The girls told their parents how they met Queen Eliza.

Printed in Great Britain
by Amazon